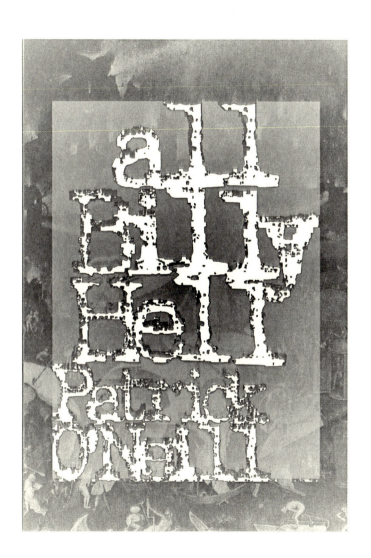

Copyright © 2010
Patrick O'Neill
March Street Press
3413 Wilshire
Greensboro NC
marchstreetpress.com
rbixby@earthlink.net
isbn 1-59661-134-0

Thanks to the editors and publishers of the following periodicals:

"Loops." *Timber Creek Review*.
"The Harlot's Beast." *The Cliffs*.
"Bed Time." *Parting Gifts*.
"Traps." *Timber Creek Review*.
"Objects Vs. Subjects." *Parting Gifts*.
"Pets." *Timber Creek Review*.
"The Comforter." *Parting Gifts*.
"On Hand." *The Cliffs*.
"The Wasp." *Parting Gifts*.
"Noise." *Parting Gifts*.
"The Masters' Words." *The Cliffs*.
"New Balance." *Parting Gifts*.
"107 (A Dog at a Time)." *Parting Gifts*.

Loops 1
The Harlot's Beast 2
Bed Time 3
Traps 6
Objects vs. Subjects 7
The Poem 9
Pets 12
Comforter 14
On Hand 17
The Wasp 18
Shelf Life 20
Glory 24
Overtyme Grill & Tap Room 26
Trolling 29
Ballet d'Action 32
Noise 33
B&E 35
Keller Drive 36
Lures 39
Feet 40
A Ways Down the Trail 41
Chase 42
Too Far North 44
The Masters' Words 47
Yards 48
Paired 50
New Balance 51
Two Plums 53
The Smile 55
Longevity 56
The Dragonflies 57
107 (A Dog at a Time) 58

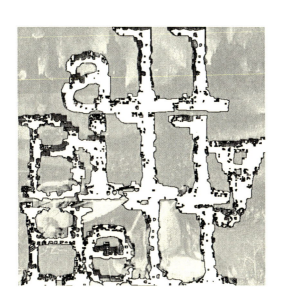

Loops

I memorize
the annular trail
by tree buds, ripe berries,
stump mushrooms, snow.
But each trek my memory—
like a defiant kid—
hightails it into the woods,
vanishes. Lost, I—
without direction, haste—
discover alien buds,
berries, mushrooms, snow—
that blow presumptions
that wandered the bygones
with me to all Billy hell.

The Harlot's Beast

A woman
told me men
fall for images,
women for stories.
That's why porn
seduces men,
soaps seduce women.

The flavorful cut
of her face,
aromatic wavelets
of her lips,
quiet lines
of her breasts,
her hips solicit me.
The Image captures,
strokes, swallows my will.

A story rises to his haunches—
howls from my bowels.

Bed Time

I sit on my bed. A friend
I teased in grade school,
fell for in high school—
who has swung
with casual mystery
in and out of my life since—
sits on my only chair.
She asks if I'm ok—
like my well-being
is hinged to marriage.
I'm not ok—but haven't been
for years, so I nod.

Aren't you lonely? *she asks.*

I think about that.
I'm living alone
for the first time
since college—
over three decades.
I slowly shake my head.
Luckily, *I say,* divorce
has chased me
into this—I swing my arm—
efficiency apartment.
And I've bonded
with the refrigerator.
I point at it—six yards away.
It hums, *I say,*
like those RC model airplanes

we built in Mr. Kern's class.
The hum rides above
deep, rhythmic moans.
This goes on for minutes
then off for minutes all night.
There's all this narrative
that on a lower level keeps
my food and beer cold.
I'd never realized refrigerators
were that talkative.

That sounds exciting, *she says*.

Ignoring the sarcasm,
I say, Yeah, it isn't often
you find a friend whose words
are custodians of your cravings.
That animates the words—
turns them into stories
that make me want
to sleep—dream.
It's like childhood bed time
when my dad read
from *Huck Finn, Tom Sawyer*.

She comes to my bed, sits next to me.
You're lonely, *she says*.

I nod.

You're horny, *she says*.

I nod.

She stands, takes off her clothes.
Why didn't you just say so? *she asks.*

I begin to undress.
I love stories, *I say.*

Here comes one, *she says,*
that will hum, moan—
maintain your cravings—
but, I hope, not put you to sleep—
at least right away.
I like my stories to linger.

Traps

As I hike down
to the Presque Isle River,
I inadvertently damage
huge spider webs.
I brush them
from my face and arms,
feeling guilty—
trying to imagine
the time, toil, ingenuity
it took to construct them
across old logging trails.
I walk on and,
like the damaged webs,
brush the guilt away—
telling myself I've sprung traps—
saving the lives of insects.

Once, I saw hundreds
of webs in a meadow
just as the morning sun
caught them carrying heavy dew.

They sparkled
like the declarations, anthems
of governments—the vows
of young lovers.

Objects vs. Subjects

Object Bites Subject

The fugitive bear,
exhausted, frightened—
staying only a few feet ahead
of the radio-collared hounds—
takes refuge in a tree.

In their vehicle,
the posse of hunters
circle the county section—
the 640-acre arena featuring
the bear's futile flight.
Barking and radio collars
monitor the chase.
When the hounds bark "treed,"
the hunters move in on foot.
One shoots the bear;
it smacks the ground.
The stunned bear rallies,
rears up, bites
the closest hunter.
The other hunters
stab the bear to death.

The headline reads:

MAN ATTACKED BY BEAR.

Subject Shoots, Stabs Object

The Animal Community Dispatch:

MEN, DOGS ATTACK, KILL BEAR

Five hunters armed
with semiautomatic
weapons and knives
in a GMC Sierra pickup,
with a tracking pack
of trained hounds, ran
to exhaustion, treed, and shot
an unarmed hundred-and-fifty-
pound black bear. The gallant,
dying bear rose up
and bit one of the hunters,
inflicting a minor wound.
The hounds leapt at the bear,
tearing his flesh,
as the other four men
stabbed the bear to death.

The Poem

The story
of the phrase's hatching
into the nest of trite figures
that sometimes flap
around in my figments
migrated to a remote site
in my early childhood.
An inquisitive friend
sent me hiking back,
flushing it out.

She was babysitting me.
Her father's handyman—
an old Romanian—
wary of her boyfriend—
said, *Watch y'r back;
drugs have made him rabid.*

She sang it to him: *I luuuv him
to beat all Bill-y hell.*

She took my hand,
headed for the door.
She whispered in my ear,
It's one of his pet phrases.
She laughed, turned, and—
like she craved its tone—
sang it again: *I luuuv him
to beat all Bill-y hell.*

His hand bade us wait.
It's a hairy way to love,
he said. *You do anything*
to beat all Billy hell
and all Billy hell trots along
like an obedient dog,
then—smack—
turns—ferocious, mad—
and wups your ass.

He became silent, sad—
twisting balled hands
in his eyes. We waited.
He finally dropped
his hands, shrugged,
said in a soft voice,
But, shit, ain't been
but one brief thing
worth beans come to me—
and she rode in,
like a bronco buster,
on my givin' 'er—
to beat all Billy hell.

I was there waving;
she left town—laughing.
When she came back,
she babysat me a few times.
She never sang,
only pretended to laugh.
Her spirit, like the story
of the stork of the phrase,

had migrated.
I tried to find it—
flush it, send it back.
But, unlike the story,
it had hidden too well
in the quagmires, brambles
of her misery.
I became weary of the hunt,
grew up, tramped recklessly
with the days and years—
lost track of her
in the quagmires, brambles
of my trek.

Pets

They're all over,
I tell my sister,
who is lamenting
her teenage son's
lackadaisical,
irresponsible lifestyle.

I see them loitering
on the peripheral
of my doing and getting done:
those young people—
stealing, begging, finagling
their fare—choosing
to grow old or die young
without knowing the rush
of stress and exertion;
the depth of sound sleep
that burrows deep
into the clay of hard work.

I look at my niece's
caged gerbil next
to my sister's
potted shamrocks
on the table we sit at.
I point, say,
There they are; it's them—
caged, potted—

*passively waiting
for the muscle and talent
of the work world
to water and feed them.*

What do we do? She asks.

I stand, raise my arms,
swing them, say,
*Turn them loose;
dump them out.*

She winces, nods, cries.

Comforter

The weight of the comforter
slowly warms the huge bed,
and drowsiness calls the image
of our German shepherd Yoda
that I just petted good night.
Instead of letting
the drowsiness have its way
and taking Yoda to sleep with me,
I turn on a canine kaleidoscope.

They all loved us—
The German shepherds
that romped through
our relationship like
the tail-waging
and snarling episodes
that harnessed us
to an uncertain,
extended bond.
There was Swartz,
the neurotic lover,
whose passion and fears
broke windows, doors—
sent us on late night searches;
Barrett, whose protective
temperament frightened away
friends until hip dysplasia
brought painful final years;
Lynkyn, whose youth, abandon
sent him in front of a speeding car;

Clancy, whose seizures,
fondness of water drowned her;
and now Yoda, whose gentle,
amusing demeanor
entertains and assures us.

Passion, possessiveness,
youthful abandon,
seizures of mistrust
painted our relationship
in a wheel of mismatched
reds and greens and blues:
striking, clashing.

Dogs love us differently;
they love us in blacks and whites.
The episodes of their lives
are less threatening to their resolves.
They're inclined to chase away
innate human-like fickleness—
making them more predictable
and less colorful than humans.

Distance, I decide,
is a tantalizing lover—
seducing us then daring
us to return to the cold,
long-empty bed of Together.

Yoda-like, I wrap myself
in that metaphor,
like the comforter
of winter nights
that seem so long ago
when we lay beneath its weight
sharing flesh and warmth—
back when more often
there was no room for Distance.

On Hand
(For Bill)

On the shore of Eel Lake,
I'm searching
for something I could
have stored
in some cubbyhole
to use to chase away
a silent distance that
that has slithered
from a disagreement
and settled between
my son and me—
when he holds out the back
of his hand and nods
at two attached dragonflies.
They're making love,
I say. *I know,* he says.
He slowly tilts his hand;
rays of sun shoot
reds, blues, greens
from their bodies.
They're beautiful, I say.
I know, he says.

The Wasp

Hurrying to teach
my one o'clock lit class,
I notice a wasp
on the floor in a corner
of an entryway, jerking
its left hind leg to free
it from a spider web.

The image stabs
into an old school bag,
jerks out a recess
on the playground
that I had silenced,
stuffed decades ago.
The Kenton brothers
hold my left leg.
I'm jerking, struggling
to get to a tiny kitten
I found shivering
under the slide.
The Kenton brothers
and Denny Knight
ganged up, took
the kitten from me.
While the brothers
keep a vice lock
on my leg, Denny
dangles the kitten
in front of me like bait.
After agonizing minutes,

Denny slams the kitten
on the ground, stomps
it to death amidst cheers—
says, *Recess is over.*

I kneel, use my office key
to cut the web as close
to the wasp's foot as I can,
coax the wasp
onto my key strap,
open the door, shake it off,
and watch it fly away.
When I turn around,
one of my students
is eyeing me curiously.

Why did you do that? she asks.

It was frightened, suffering.

It might sting someone, she says.

Or it might pollinate something, I say.

Laughing, she says, *It's fall.*
Things are dying.
You should have killed the sonofabitch.

Shelf Life

Enjoying the Caribbean landscape,
I wind along the resort beach
between blankets and lounges
that showcase mostly nearly naked
American and European women,
cooking themselves in the sun.
I pass the last blanket
where a young, topless blonde
rolls from her stomach to her back
and smiles at me. I linger.
She's overcooked—brown
to the verge of black.
It's a nice color
but doesn't go with her hair.
Thinking of basting,
sticking a meat thermometer
in her, I smile, wave, and head
off the beach to a trail.
It weaves through palm trees—
discarded appliances, other junk—
takes me to Puerto Aventuras.

A little above and beyond
the dolphin marina—
the centerpiece of town—is
The Pub, owned by a guy from Wisconsin.
A huge Budweiser banner reads,
WELCOME SNOWMOBILERS.

In Michigan, she managed
the Colonel Sanders
I was painting. She backed
a delivery truck into my ladder,
knocked me off. We bonded—
became a couple.
She's behind an empty bar.
Doesn't seem surprised.
We freeze, stare at each other.
She's still blonde—
but now, medium well done.
She says, *Well? Have I changed?*

You've cooked yourself some.

*That's hard not to do
around here. Besides,
those years at the Colonel's,
have come back to haunt me.*
I point at the tap; she draws a draft.

Corona? I ask.

She shakes her head. *Sol.
Probably a better beer—
a little cheaper.
People assume it's Corona—*
she waves her hands
at the Corona signs—
because of all the hype.

Most hard-core Corona drinkers
want bottles—with a lime.
It's a good thing—
the lime. The clear bottles
make the beer go skunky—
short shelf life.

A man comes from the back,
says, *Hey.* She goes to him.
He whispers; she whispers.
They smile, nod. He leaves,
waving a money pouch at us.

She comes back—
looks like she might cry.
I stand, finish my beer.
I shouldn't have come.
I want to say something funny
about craving a lime.

I skulk along the marina,
watching dolphins tow people
and jump through hoops. I pause
in front of Gringo Dave's,
think about stopping for a beer—
sitting, watching the dolphins
earn their fish—but continue
to the beach, thinking *North*—
snowmobiles, skis, snowshoes.

On the trail, trying to stay
in the stingy shade of palms,
I bond with abandoned kin:
a refrigerator, a sink—
I stop at a gimped stove,
its oven handle twisted
in a grimace. I pat it, inhale.
Trans fats, that add shelf life
to Kentucky fried chicken
and golden cuts of caring,
mingle with old Corona—
without the lime.
Ahead at the beach,
I glimpse the well-done blonde.
I wonder if she's on her back
or—if she's on her stomach—
if she'll roll over for me.

Glory

Maybe, *I say*,
rummaging for ammunition
in the past for an attack
in the future is keeping
you too busy to build
something in the present.

There is no present, *she says*.
The instant something happens
it becomes the past.

That instant—that flash—
is the present, *I say*.

She says, But we can only
imagine that flash. We have
to connect what happened
to what's going to happen.

Right, *I say*. We walk the edge
of the past and future.
Moments of agony, ecstasy
hold us to the edge.
But when they release us,
we have to give her all Billy hell
to stay on trail—get to camp.

You're too far
to the left,
lugging things
too far to the right.

She says, but so is he.
It's the only way
I can win the war.

I say, if you both walked the edge,
you wouldn't be at war.

That's like saying, *she says,*
if we all walked the edge
there wouldn't be war.

That's right, *I say.*

Get real, *she says.*
No combat
no glory.
I'll skip camp—
kill the snake!

OverTyme
Grill & Tap Room

I walk back to the bar
from peering out the window
at the caboose of a sunny day:
an avocado cloud bank
trying like hell to break
loose from the horizon.
A wandering waitress
falls in step with me,
asks, *Checking out
the beautiful weather?*

I say, *I hate sun.*

No. Really, she says.
*You can't hate sun.
No one hates sun.*

I do.

You should move to Seattle,
she says.

I think about it, I say.

She walks to a coworker,
swings her head at me—whispers.

They look at me; I raise my beer
to them, take a sip.

Awhile later, the coworker
comes to the bar, says,
I bet you're not big on parades.

No tolerance for them, I say.

Weddings?

Ugly spectacles.

Fairs?

Same thing.

What do you like?

Rain, a woman, a cold beer.

You know, she says,
I'll bet we could get along.

Yeah, I say. *Where you from?*

Hawaii. She points
at the window. *Look*, she says,
the sun's going away.

I watch an avocado tint
spread across the window.

Listen! she says.

Long, low rumbling—
like the deep complaint
of disgruntled bowels—
a thunder clap pump us,
have us smiling, gawking
at each other like kids
until the other waitress
calls her, points to her table—
and she pulls away.

I turn to my beer, wonder,
watch the rain begin
to pelt the window.

Trolling
(For Beth Grbavcich)

Juggling the smile, energy
of a young instructor along
with the souths, wests
of her directions
and her Missouri laugh
as I wave off her offer
to escort me to US 41,
I'm driving around lost
on the outskirts
of the Northern Michigan campus—
where I had just opened
a door of my poetry,
let out people, images
for a large group
of college freshmen.
Along with my juggling,
clusters of reactions—
disbelief, confusion,
defiance, indifference—
drive around aimlessly,
bump into each other,
the juggling—create a heap.
She knows: I drive my car
like I drive my poetry.
I don't know where
the fuck I'm going. I'm not
a responsible chauffeur.

A tiny man peeks
over a podium, taunts me:
Plan the trip; buckle
your words in; watch the road,
read the signs. I nod,
ignore what he says.

I stop where three men
are building a basement.
They smile up at me
from the deep hole
where they're working
on lower tiers of blocks.
Distance turns them tiny;
I think of trolls—exiled
for laughing, loving.
I'm lost, I explain.
They scramble
up a ladder, each
with his own directions.
In no hurry to return
to their toil, they debate
whose directions
will be quickest, easiest to follow.

They study architects'
detailed plans, lay blocks—
build foundations, structures
that will keep houses standing,
people dry, warm, safe.
I think of my labor:
Without plans, I lay words

in jumbled piles that mock
foundations, structures—
shove shelter seekers
into the rain, snow, cold—
scuttle security.
I've never found a reason
to obey blueprints, maps—
never learned to read them.

In my rear-view mirror
the trolls are on the road,
waving wildly, pointing south.

I miss my first turn.

Ballet d'Action

Water striders dance
on the pool below the dam.
Sometimes a hungry creek chub
catches one in a brusque pause,
snaps it off the calm surface.

Appétit pour la vie
glides, swirls the bugs—
incessant, stark—
among their living, till death
performs his *Ballet d' Coup*.

Noise

What's that noise? she asks.

I listen. It's three things, I say.

Three things?

I nod. I hear a mouse
in the wall, the wind slapping
a branch against the house,
and the hum of the refrigerator.

It's *that* branch? It's terrible.
I thought you cut it off.

Why? It has a novel beat—
that pilots the nomadic beauty.

Beauty? What's beautiful?

Disorganized noise, I say.
It's spontaneous—
honest, revealing—
unlike manipulated noises
of language and music.
Last evening, I listened
to a woods getting ready for bed:
the breeze gradually softening
the rustling of tree leaves,
coyotes singing, squirrels scolding,
crows cawing, doves cooing.

This morning I listened
to a city getting out of bed:
garbage cans clanging,
pigeons cooing, walkways stirring,
traffic swelling, a dog barking.
Learn to appreciate
the stark stories
of disorganized noise—
as unrehearsed as screams
of agony and ecstasy.

We can skip the agony,
get ready for bed, and play
some of those screams
of ecstasy, she says—
if you'll promise
to get organized, get rid
of that branch tomorrow—
and while you're at it,
set a mouse trap.

B&E
(For Laurel)

A confirmed
mother, sister, mistress
to her plants tells me
last fall she displayed
birdhouses on a shelf
in the attached garage.
In early spring,
she hears thumping—
a mystery until Mother's Day
when birds—like quack grass
storming her garden plots—
swarm her garage.
The bandits lodge
in her houses, raise families
without paying rent—
claim the premises
as a training/dumping ground
before skedaddling south.
The spirit and independence
of invading weeds, birds, animals
shows that function tutors decoration
because naked, organic instinct
kicks the Billy hell out of pretense.

Keller Drive

A stranger named Keller
bought an interior forty
in a heavily wooded corner
of the township.
He built a shack on it,
demanded road access.
So the county
built him a road.
Keller, who lived
more like a beast than
a culture-broken human,
stayed out of sight
except for infrequent
bicycle trips to town
where he'd drink,
go wild, sometimes spend
a night in the county cage.
People treated the crude man
like a large,
semidomesticated animal—
observing his entertaining,
carnal behavior from a distance.

A year after they authorized
the building of the road,
the county board decided
to give it a name
and put it on the June agenda.
They were about to unanimously
award the honor to a fellow

who had lived in the area
for over fifty years
and hadn't bothered anyone
when Keller ambled in—
like a dump bear—
and gruffly recommended
they name the road after him.
He reminded them he was
the reason there was a road.
The wilderness about him
visibly unstrung
the board members.
They tried to table
the recommendation.
Keller grunted, shook his head—
suggested a roll-call vote.

It was seven-zilch.
Somehow Keller Drive
had just become a memorial
to a debauchee who
hung out with the animals
and mocked the people
who had just honored him.
An older timer than me
capped it nicely over a beer
after the meeting.

It's funny, he said,
how ignorance and fear
of things like the untamed
can often snatch

small and large pieces
of immortality away
from where you'd likely
think they'd best fit—
and put them
where you're later apt
to agree they belong.

Lures

I'll do anything for you,
we said—*anything.*
Beautiful. But that's
what killed it.
Remember the colorful
oriental bittersweet
you showed me
that decorates the trunks
of strong, healthy trees—
while slowly girdling them?
Look at the pledges
of patriots that decorate
the rooted trunks of nations
while sucking away
the freedoms, well-being
of the patriots. So, too often,
the promises of friends,
the vows of young lovers,
are warm, attractive decoys
that we crave, embrace
as the disguised assassins
lovingly entwine—choke, kill.

Feet

She tells me feet
kick her spring in the ass.
They boot out the joys
of resurrection. Feet bring
March, April, May, June
mud into her house:
feet of people
she tries to care about—
people who pay no attention
to her pleas to go Japanese—
people who walk around half naked
but won't take their shoes or boots off.

They tramp through the kitchen,
living room of her being.

A Ways Down the Trail

A green kid
just out of junior high,
I'm hiking to Cherry Creek
with old man O'Conner.
He's taking me to a secret place
where hardly anyone fishes
and the brookies strike and scrap
like Lake Gogebic smallmouths.
Along the way, I ask him,
*When am I going to know
what the hell I'm going to be?*

He says, *You'll find out in a while.*

When's a while? I ask.

He almost smiles, nods ahead,
says, *It's a ways down the trail.*

Since, I've walked many trails
to wade new streams—
casting the question,
anticipating hooking the answer
around each alien bend—
knowing old man O'Conner
a ways back up the trail
already hooked and landed
that phantom fish for me.

Chase

We watch two squirrels
high in the maples
put on an acrobatic show.
They race, leap
from tree to tree
from the top-most branches
that bend like drawn bows
but never break.
They're playing, I think,
probably tag. But my girl—
an animal authority—
tells me they're mating.

Wow! I say. *What a way
to go after a woman!
Does that mean
when he catches her
he keeps her?*

For a while, she says. *They jump
from squirrel to squirrel
like they leap from tree to tree.*

Infidels, I say.

She says, *Yeah. It's what keeps
them such a hardy bunch.
It's genetically sound behavior.
It keeps their offspring healthier.*

I'll be damned, I say.
*An argument for fucking around.
Look at the problems they avoid:
divorce, custody battles.*

She says, *You're no squirrel.
If you recall, your courting
was stumble-creep not race-leap.
I felt more like a field vet
than a fleeing female.*

It was a strategy, I say lamely.

She gives me a look.
It's all right, she says.
We do fine on the lower limbs.

Too Far North

We were lovers
before she split south.
Now she's back—
turns me tutor (with fringes)—
to show her how
to put words together
with punctuation marks
and stuff them in paragraphs
well enough to pass
her law-school entry essay.

She asks, *If you don't
ski or snowmobile or snowshoe,
why are you staying
in the frigid upper peninsula
of Michigan?*

I don't ice fish either, I say.
*I do brood and bitch.
But I think it's good for me;
it tempers me—keeps me in shape
for all the shit that—
like misused punctuation marks—
muddle the metric of who I am.*

We drive six hundred miles
to the southeast lower peninsula.
The next morning I go to a park,
sit by a pond to do paperwork.
A white bird tiptoes

through the water, only feet
in front of me.
Something albino, rare—
to put on a page of my day.
It freezes, shapes its neck
like a question mark,
strikes the water like a period,
straightens its neck
into an exclamation point
while swallowing
a flapping minnow,
that thrashes down
the exclamation point
to the sudden stop. I watch
seven fascinating sequels.

Excited, I tell her
about the rare bird.

She laughs. *An egret,*
she says.
They're common.
Are you going to admit
you live too far north?

Up north, I say,
there's no question.
It would have been
an exclamation point
in anyone's chapter.
Period.

So would a penguin down here!
she says. Or a polar bear!
Exclamation point!

I say, *Guess I'll head north,*
hunt camels, comma.

The Masters' Words

Once they roared like whitecaps,
washed over me, around me,
then ran into gutters,
settled into stagnant pools—
sometimes pelted me
like stones, bounced off,
lolled in random piles.

I visit the pools, the piles.
I swirl the pools with my hands,
stir the piles with my feet—
wait: nothing. Dejected,
I go back to my puddles
and miniature mounds—
search for motion, sound—
find stillness, silence.
I prospect for energy—
pan some—spend it
to roil the water,
propel the stones.
Then I steep
in the feeble ripples,
clutch the laggard lobs.

Yards

She's old, alone—
over the years, I've counted
two live-in lovers she's had.
Her neighbors have
multiplied them by several.
They count on her
to feed the gossip roaming
neighborhood yards.
My mother told me
they call her Rainy Day
because one rainy day
she mentioned
to her meter reader
she'd rather wake up
to rain than sun.

On this visit
to the neighborhood,
I stand in sub-zero
temperatures and admire
her yard ornaments.
A woman, bent, daffodils
in her left hand,
grapples in deep snow
with her right hand for more;
a flamingo, up to his butt
in snow, gazes in wonderment
out over the whiteness;
a girl in shorts, sunbonnet
waters the snow-covered yard

with a tiny watering can.
It's like the images—frozen—
wait for warm weather
to spring them to life.
It might be Rainy Day forgot
to take them in or doesn't care.
But she well could have left
them as emblems
of the neighbors' minds
frozen in yards
of biased judgments.

I look at the flamingo;
he looks at me;
his eyes plead. *Okay,* I say,
and I bet she's lonely.
I walk into the yard,
wiggle the flamingo loose
from the frozen snow.
As I pull him out, I say,
You know, Phoenix,
you're mocking a legend.
We look for you to rise
from fire—not ice.

We head up the walk,
knock on the door.

Paired

I count them: ten geese,
thirty-eight goslings—
along the edge
of a Waterford park pond,
the goslings resting
between paired parents.
There are nine goslings
with the pair nearest me.
One goose sleeps
standing on one leg,
the other sits—alert.

My cell phone rings.
My wife tells me
the kids are fine.
She says it's all set.
We're going to try
to make it work
with one lawyer
when I return.

It's like when we were a pair;
I feel her there with me,
touching my arm, laughing
at the goslings waking up,
stretching their legs.
I say, *Geese mate for life.*

She asks if I've been drinking.

New Balance

For firm footing,
I cinch my laces, double-bow
my New Balance shoes.
I head out on my 4:30 A.M.
six-mile run that I trick myself
into suffering three days a week.
In late fall, at this early hour,
without a moon,
before winter drops
its luminous tarp,
it's blacker than all Billy hell
on the back roads of Ironwood.
Dreading another day
of facing sluggish lit classes,
searching old folders for ways
to prod the students,
I round a Norrie curve,
lifting my feet high
to keep from tripping
in invisible pot holes—
when I stumble
over a waddling skunk.
Glimpsing the white stripe
continuing across the road,
I catch my balance,
sprint. Too late.
Thick odor chokes, chases me—
like a rabid animal.
I hold my breath off and on,
cursing the vaporous beast.

I sprint for a few yards,
then slow, let it catch me.
But it's no longer a threat.
Breathing normally, I
tolerate the stench.
Another mile and I relocate
my sense of humor.
The stench becomes an aroma;
we run along together—
joking, laughing. At the end
of the run we're friends.
I inhale deeply, thank him
for the company.
I shower, dress—it hits me:
my friend, the prod. I debate,
then put on—lace loosely, tie—
the New Balance shoes.
My friend lingers,
a sniff of what he was.
He of course comes
to classes with me.
In his diminished state,
he's still dynamic—
drawing students
into poems, stories, plays
who usually—
in untied, no-tie shoes—
stumble, sprint, circumnavigate
far from them.

Two Plums

The farm, my wife, and I had
a twenty-two year affair.
Goodbye is rough.
The animals, the kids are gone.
But trees I planted still stand.
I visit them for the last time.

Two ten-year-old apple trees
shrug, show me
unripe August apples.
A spruce I planted for shade
by the pond—tall, complacent—
gazes out over the water—
like a lighthouse
with nothing to do.
Four firs show off their height—
three taller than I am.
Younger maples, a weeping birch
wave in a breeze at each other.
The youngest, an apple tree,
my fourth attempt
to grow a tree in memory
of my father-in-law—
surviving two years
of deer, heavy snow—
seems caught up
in the dream of becoming
what my father-in-law wanted:
a large, sturdy tree—
full of apples

for kids to climb for.
The last tree
I almost forget, walk by.
It grew away
from conifer shade—
crooked, bent—
like something born already old.
It never gave a decent yield.
This year, it was
a snow storm of blossoms
when mid-May frost
gutted it. I give it a wave,
begin to move on—
something stops me.
I turn, walk closer—eyes.
Two plums peer out at me
from among the leaves—
the only two on the tree.
I stare back. A quick breeze
rattles leaves—the tree says,
You and I share a story.
We grew differently,
fought for worthy yields—
gave what we could.
Thanks for the years.
What the hell! Here.
It's the best I can do.
I walk over.

With humble hands,
I pick two ripe, firm plums.

The Smile

In a restaurant,
I watch a smile
fastened to a man's face
as he sermonizes
to three attentive women
his contempt for gays
and a state politician
who advocates
insurance coverage
for gay couples.
The smile never
goes away, fades—
even when he speaks.
He carries it to the restroom,
brings it back to the table.

I wonder if he took it off
in there, maybe let it
rest, relieve, groom itself—
or if it's as firmly fixed
as the color of his skin,
the shape of his skull,
the set of his mind.

Longevity

A Native American
told me her grandfather
cut a moon-counting stick
every spring. At the rising
of first moons—thirteen
on the Sioux calendar—
he'd notch it. New light,
he'd say. It rejuvenates
buffalo—us. He watched
his constitution sprout
forked tongues;
his small dairy farm
collapse under costly
government regulations;
his children
turn to drugs, crime—
die in needless wars;
the buffalo diminish.

Without doctors, medications,
he stayed healthy, useful
for a hundred-and-one years—
counting moons on collected sticks.

The Dragonflies

I watch two dragonflies
make love on a dogwood leaf
that a breeze swings
over the river,
in and out of the shade—
several others as they fly.
Many—unattached—
glide above, beneath,
ogle the coupling
like reconnaissance planes.

There are no closed bedroom doors,
back seats on dark, dead-end roads;
nor is there exhibition—
only a candor as grand
as the greens, reds, and blues
of their shimmering bodies
as they oscillate from shade to sun.

107 (A Dog at a Time)

She left in a hurry
tossing a hasty goodbye
to her daughter and the dog,
the last dog of four.

In her eighties,
she began rescuing
dogs from the shelter—
one dog at a time—
to mitigate her daughter's
ache of living alone.

Three died of old age.

A massive coronary strolled in
as if it had overlooked something—
and took her while she was sorting
her spring clothes for mending.